The Most Kissed Woman in the World

The Most Kissed Woman in the World

Poems by

Patricia Caspers

© 2024 Patricia Caspers. All rights reserved.
This material may not be reproduced in any form, published,
reprinted, recorded, performed, broadcast,
rewritten, or redistributed without
the explicit permission of Patricia Caspers.
All such actions are strictly prohibited by law.

Cover design by Shay Culligan
Cover photo "Fair Trade Frame of Mind" by Duy Huynh
Author photo by Rick Ross

ISBN: 978-1-63980-551-8

Kelsay Books
502 South 1040 East, A-119
American Fork, Utah 84003
Kelsaybooks.com

For the Unitarian Universalists who offer me clean drinking water every time I'm lost in the woods.

Thanks

I am grateful to have more people to thank for supporting this book than it's possible to name in this space. Here are a few:

Thank you to Karen Kelsay, Jenna Wray, and everyone else at Kelsay Books for saying yes a second time and for treating my poems with such care.

Thank you to Jennifer Martelli and Chloe Martinez for the kind words and to Duy Huynh for the beautiful cover art.

Thank you to my poetry bestie, Annie Stenzel, for the wise words and big laughs.

Thank you to my many, many workshoppers over the years for their support and brilliance, including; Lisa Ahn, Katherine Case, Jessica Del Pozo, Renato Gasparetti, Laura Grodrian, Irene Lipshin, Moira Magneson, Jennifer K. Sweeney, Jenifer Vernon, Wendy Williams, and Claire Unis.

Thank you to Cynthia Della Penna, Molly Dunham, and Dana Ross for the inspirational conversation and support.

Thank you to my many professors at Sierra College, Chico State University, and Mills College (RIP), for the kindness and generosity.

Thank you to my Unitarian Universalist friends who helped inspire these poems and to my friend Jennifer Peart for introducing me to Octavia E. Butler.

Finally, thank you to my family—Rick, Jacob, Olivia, Seamus, Mom, and Gary—for gifting me with the time and love needed to write these words.

Acknowledgments

I send my gratitude to the kind editors and staff at the journals where the following poems originally appeared, sometimes in previous iterations:

Abandon Journal: "Portrait of God as Deer in the Compost Pile"
Arc Poetry Magazine: "Portrait of God as How to Find Cleaning Drinking Water in the Woods"
Border Crossing: "Portrait of God as Sierra Nevada Watershed"
Cider Press: "Portrait of God as Facebook Page of a Deceased Friend"
Cimarron Review: "Portrait of God as High-Five After Making Love"
Crab Creek Review: "Portrait of God as My Intention to Write a Poem About the Day My Love Became a Cyborg"
Kestrel: "Portrait of God as Bottle of Urine in a Ditch Beside Applegate Frontage Road," "Portrait of God as Damp Dishtowel," "Portrait of God as This Twelve-Year-Old Girl"
Literary Mama: "Portrait of God as the Beginning"
Malahat Review: "Portrait of God as Making Love in the Time of Pandemic"
Night Heron Barks: "Portrait of God as Girl Ginkgo"
Rust + Moth: "Portrait of God as Mother Weather"
Sugar House Review: "Portrait of God as Seasons and Limits"
Terrain.org: "Portrait of God as Glittering of Hummingbirds"
UCity Review: "Portrait of God as Mission Fig and Female Fig Wasp," "Portrait of God as Most Kissed Woman in the World"
Whale Road Review: "Portrait of God as American Assisted Living Facility," "Portrait of God as Mother Stegosaurus"

Contents

I

Portrait of God as Deer in the Compost Pile	17
Portrait of God as Girl Ginkgo	19
Portrait of God as Mother Stegosaurus	20
Portrait of God as Aggregate of Manatees	21
Portrait of God as 52 Blue	22
Portrait of God as Mission Fig & Female Fig Wasp: a Dialogue	23
Portrait of God as Facebook Page of a Deceased Friend	25
Portrait of God as a Bottle of Urine in a Ditch Beside Applegate Frontage Road	26
Portrait of God as California Wildfire	27
Portrait of God as Shadow of a Woman Riding a Bike Through Blue Oak Savannah	28
Portrait of God as How to Find Clean Drinking Water in the Woods	29
Portrait of God as Sierra Nevada Watershed	30
Portrait of God as Glittering of Hummingbirds	31
Portrait of God as December Haiku Ending in Baubles	32
Portrait of God as Wintertide	33

II

Portrait of God as Most Kissed Woman in the World	37
Portrait of God as This Twelve-Year-Old Girl	38
Portrait of God as Ode to Panties (Remix)	39
Portrait of God as First Kiss	40
Portrait of God as Ruth in Boaz's Fields	41
Portrait of God as a Woman Like That (Remix)	42

Portrait of God as Golden Shovel Ending in Poet's Own Words	43
Portrait of God as Worten's Market	44
Portrait of God as the Artist's Regret	46
Portrait of God as Keeper of Keys	47
Portrait of God as Words with Friends with Your Father's Second of Three Wives: A One Line Golden Shovel	48
Portrait of God as Jolene's Response (Remix)	49
Portrait of God as Dysfunctional Family	50
Portrait of God as Mother Weather	51
Portrait of God as Your Mother Offering to Gift You a Gun	52
Portrait of God as American Assisted Living Facility	53
Portrait of God as Contemplation of Suicide While Driving Highway 80 and After Reading Pema Chödrön	55
Portrait of God as Gas Station Haiku	56
Portrait of God as Field Notes from a Small-Town Reporter	57
Portrait of God as Seasons and Limits	58
Portrait of God as Ars Poetica with Ghosts	60

III

Portrait of God as the Beginning	63
Portrait of God as One Saturday in September	64
Portrait of God as Daughter Cooking Ddukbokki	65
Portrait of God as Daughter	66
Portrait of God as My Son's Epistaxis	67
Portrait of God as the Space in My Mouth Where My Front Teeth Once Lived	68

Portrait of God as Popcorn Kernel	69
Portrait of God as Middle-Aged Woman in the Shower	70
Portrait of God as a Marriage Haiku	72
Portrait of God as Damp Dish Towel	73
Portrait of God as Gold Wedding Band	75
Portrait of God as Lovemaking in the Time of Pandemic	76
Portrait of God as My Intention to Write a Poem About the Day My Love Became a Cyborg—	77
Portrait of God as Supermarket Haiku	78
Portrait of God as High-Five After Making Love	79

I

The universe is God's self-portrait
—Octavia E. Butler

Portrait of God as Deer in the Compost Pile

Though it's drought season
and every very thing is dead yellow, and the sun
doesn't feel like friend,
I spend all day on the deck
with a fan, a laptop, and a cup of ice water.
I tap at the alphabet while a single deer
taps at the dirt beyond the brush
on the far side of the tree line.
He's skinny, and his antlers
are nubs, dusty cattails, and slowly
he hooves closer. As I stretch
we catch eyes—mine blue predator;
his, autumn prey.
He stands still for so long he seems
to have forgotten what he's about,
but then takes tentative steps
toward the slop in the bin, begins
to nibble a half mango gone rotten,
dangles a day-old banana peel
from his narrow mouth.
It retracts like a bruised tongue.
His own tongue is sunset pink as he nudges
a mushy red apple from beneath
the coffee grounds, grasps it
between front teeth and nods
the way my favorite yellow lab
does with his chewed bone.
Between each deer bite there's caution
and stillness at the shout of neighbor dogs,
the scatter of lizard feet through dry grass,
the twir of a lost hummingbird—each
a possible danger—and his pauses
remind me of something in myself.

My friend Annie doesn't like deer and curses
when she spots them in the yard, even the fawns
with their polka dot coats, even after all
Stafford had to say on the matter.
I can't help but admire them
though it's mostly stags come this side
of the canyon and eat the few veggies
we manage not to burn. This deer—
my new friend, for he looks me over
and does not run—has a filmy white something
I want to rub from the dark path of his eyes,
and hedge-parsley burs caught between
the tuning antennae of his ears.
Minutes pass, and he samples the lettuce—gone to seed
in the neglected raised beds, bitter
probably—and dashes suddenly, disappears
behind scrub oaks. Are we the same,
dear friend, I wonder, as I return to fatten my page
on the detritus of other stolen gardens.

Portrait of God as Girl Ginkgo

Before words, there was a cool slake of river,
the depths I quarried, and the silver eddies
where I shucked each spent leaf—
amber fluke, tattered wing of swallowtail—
the silt cradle where a single blade might press
its shadow into the firmament.

You complain of my creature odor,
name the scent *vomit, semen,*
but I blossom green as spring, grow
golden with summershine, orbit
my own self with small, dazzling suns—
and if their ripening into the future
offends your human senses, I am not sorry.

Come glacier, come tiger moth, come beetle, come
fission, come Adam with concrete and smog,
the workworn hands that bind my roots
in shallow city boxes, fingers that each autumn
gather my seeds from where they land on the asphalt
where there once was a river.

Portrait of God as Mother Stegosaurus

Except that I build
hatchlings from marrow, except
rivals gnash and pierce one another's skulls
for the pleasure of my body
except that I am yet, sapling
unfinished, ringing into my own possibility
when the future is demanded of me
except that I am armor
and will not be taken by whim or deceit—
what do they see in my inner architecture,
except the endling in themselves?

Portrait of God as Aggregate of Manatees

Barnacle-scarred in brackish shallows,
manatees don algae-green sweaters and circle
sweet seagrass. Submarines, we see in them,
elephants, cows, mermaids who tempt—swish of tail—
the homesick mariner from his vessel.
While we symbol their wrinkled bodies, while we
strap their peduncles and divine their patterns
rippling the surface tension, manatees graze
and glide gracefully, mating, or perhaps
pulling a latched nursling nestled under fin,
tide-rising by the power of their own digestion.
We—the manatees' only predator—work steadily
to save them as we serve them toxic blooms, motor blades,
ghost line. We monitor manatee distress, write it
in our notebooks, how they lift the injured,
their dying kind.

Portrait of God as 52 Blue

her lost language slips
through star traps, below sun prows
sea as universe

Portrait of God as Mission Fig & Female Fig Wasp: a Dialogue

Fat-bellied men
in pointy hats

                        We are starful
                        in our plentitude

batwing scrotums
sexy when ripe

                        beckoned by an echo of scent
                        feverfish in flight, pollen-light

squeeze us into any box
we take its shape

                                  disinterested in sting
                                  we burrow

turn us on our side
we're platypusian

                        into the sweet and meaty heart
                        that sustains you

one father tried
to namesake us

                              the journey a severing
                              we sacrifice our wings

palmed us over
along with a pox

                              eschew escape
                              pirouette the ever-after

but we are thousands
floral mycelium

                                        shade-gathering
                                        hands pluck the tender fruit

we blossom inside ourselves,
invite death, melt all danger

                                        sun warm and sticky
                                        fear-pressed, your lips

on our wet, pink tongues   our work, awaiting joy

Portrait of God as Facebook Page of a Deceased Friend

Who will tell,
as year in, year out,
the algorithm reminds them
to wish you happy birthday,
and they are not bothered
by your continual non-reply,
as you were never
one to dazzle a cocktail party,
belly laugh, guffaw,
but content to quiet corners,
and so they are pleased
with their triple heart emojis,
despite the long absence,
and you are
that philosophical tree—
redwood, perhaps?—
deep in a forest grove,
fallen log we pass unnoticed,
home to grouse, ants,
clustered sulfur tuft,
ever silent.

Portrait of God as a Bottle of Urine in a Ditch Beside Applegate Frontage Road

I began as a blessing of rain that watered the apricot tree, or gathered to circle the chambers of a beast's heart, or perhaps was gathered to quench the thirst of a milking cow, sweeten the cream of the coffee you sip while flipping between stations in the sedan, the pickup, the semi that carries you home, to work on the mountain, to play in its dearth of snow, or carries you farther East, away from the life you were promised, or the life you promised another. I was separated from myself in the red embryo, island pillow of the kidneys, as you separate yourself from where you have been, cleave toxins, the faceless drivers in the cars beside you in the night, separate from your own body, the weight of you there in the seat, the surety of the belt pressed against your chest, as you fiddle with the dials to heat the air that warms your legs, colder with elevation. The length of the urethra is the motorway I travel, as you steer this highway, perhaps a little too fast, and I am you, always filling, always asking that you stop and notice, pause for this moment, and any other night you would rest for this ritual of letting go, but time is not itself lately, and the glass bottle beside you is empty, and isn't it beautiful how golden we are, there, in the littered gully, below the branches of the madrone tree, where we glitter in passing headlights— as though the moon is not enough—home now, where only the most curious coyote will find us.

Portrait of God as California Wildfire

The origin is mystery: chain scrapes asphalt, sparks leap
a pickup's undercarriage, smoulder drought grass, hidden smoke.

Cigarette versus oxygen tank, which is to say addiction, or pain
that burns like a scorned lover's letters gone ash, gone smoke.

Neglected bonfire, or warming fire when camp is necessity not
leisure, when tents blossom beside a river and disperse like smoke.

One spring a young god camped along the mudbank, caught a fire,
tossed flames into water. Undoused, it eddied like smoke.

Years later, god hiked a burned mountain, charred pines, blackened
needles, cindered soil, found surprise: the hearth scent of smoke.

Portrait of God as Shadow of a Woman Riding a Bike Through Blue Oak Savannah

She's flying almost
silver silk
over sunburned grasses,
Gold Rush tailings,
scrub brush. Turkeys
scatter with her
change of light,
toss pearled feathers
to the wind.
A covey of quail
bark as she slivers
close branches.
Some days the rider
falls into the shadow
some days away,
while the sun,
a sleepy river,
winds around
flickering wheels.
The shadow doesn't need it,
the sun.
She doesn't need
that barrel-chested moon,
or even a streetlamp.
Her breath darkens dust
stirred by tires
as she listens for the crack
of another acorn.
The rider will weary,
cycle home again,
garage the machine,
and the shadow god follows,
but stays behind, too—floats
through the night woods.

Portrait of God as How to Find Clean Drinking Water in the Woods

First you have to say to your mind, say,
Girlfriend, be quiet for once in your goddamn life.
She won't listen—you know—but maybe
she'll hear it anyhow, the chatter, prattle,
gibberish of water-splashed granite. You want
a creek is what you want. You want kindness
of frog spawn, of water skippers, of minnow lurk.
Don't drink that water! Don't ask yourself
what in hell caused you to be solitary
in the wilderness without one sweet swallow.
What you wouldn't give for a ginger beer, a cola,
even the strawberry Kool-Aid Grandma
served in pale pastel tumblers,
plastic cups you snuck again and again to the stream
down the red clay hill where you collected pollywogs fat
as glistening apostrophes,
but there was no owning that magic of growing fast.
Forge blackberry and its vicious thorns, tangles of ivy.
Your kidneys will fail, your brain will shrink—*Girlfriend, please.*
When the water is a trickle, a tickle from the source,
seek the place where it laughs at itself, clasp
your hands together and, *Girlfriend I mean it,* pray for rain.

Portrait of God as Sierra Nevada Watershed

Native Americans settled for thousands of years in the Truckee Valley. Their camps were on these flats near the river. They used fish blinds near here and left petroglyphs on boulders.
—Nevada Historical Marker

What was the meaning of "settle"
to men who arrived mud-creased,
boot-broken, afoul of snow, tobacco poor?
They named that which was never nameless:
beaver, river, fish, peak.
And what they saw they took.
Such easy game, the beaver—*su-i'-tu-ti-kut-teh'*—
so simple to slip a hand under brook water and strangle.
They wanted the river, too, named the current
for cutthroat salmon that thrived in its pools and then
fished those salmon into memory.
Again settlers courted the water,
called it *Truckee,* after the Paiute chief
whose true name baffled their tongues.
Chief Tru-ki-zo guided these gold hungry men
away from the flow of his namesake
as it travels one hundred miles from Tahoe basin,
fishhooks north and east to Pyramid Lake
where the Virginia Mountains, the Pah Pah Range
and the Smoke Creek Desert
cradle each drop in their dry embrace.
Still the ancient river, as aloof as the red-tailed hawk,
slips into sky, becomes rain.

Portrait of God as Glittering of Hummingbirds

We are a fever of ruby gorget, a streak
of smoke-filtered sun on a cloudless morning

We are not the names you've given us

We are cups of cattail and willow,
wolf silk, moth silk, lichen and moss

We are nestled in a crook of blue oak,
delighting in the understory

We climb the silver ladder of sky,
plummet and trill our desire

We are window reflection,
tabby's paw, weight of bumblebee

We are all the names you've given us

We are bright nectar dilating the map of home,
autumn's sudden frost

Portrait of God as December Haiku Ending in Baubles

Dirt furrows, barren
under stone sky—look closely
onion red glimmer

Portrait of God as Wintertide

It's never too cold to snow
once a snowflake
dissolves to rain, it won't
become neve again
in its lifetime
birch mushrooms
shelf more than their share
of schnee against
a moon-silver evening
yuki no hana falls
from a slightly
sun-struck sky,
and the tiniest flakes
create themselves
without the froth
of cloud cover
the geometry
of traffic lines
is obscured by apun:
drive where you like
the sharpest air
holds little water;
expect few crystals,
faux neige
unutsi is art
that never points
in fewer than six directions
imagine earth a single crust
blackberry pie,
your helping heavy
with whipped cream,
and nature a grandmother
Mangia, mangia, she scolds
we must fatten you up

II

I found God in myself, and I loved her/ I loved her fiercely
 —Ntozake Shange

Portrait of God as Most Kissed Woman in the World

Workmen pulled your body from that green turn of river,
and push or jump, no one could say, and no one
claimed you until the death doctor anointed your face with oil
applied thin threaded layers of plaster, the scent of wet dust
rising into the morgue. The plaster became the shape of your
cheekbones, your brow, the secret on your lips.
Soon, wax filled the place where your face had been.

We gave you names: *Unknown Woman, Drowned Woman, Woman of Sorrows, Woman of Many Fears, Woman Who Was Pushed or Woman Who Didn't Want to Die, but Didn't Want to Live This Life, Woman Who Was Only a Girl, Resusci Annie.*

Forgive us; we hung your face on our walls.
Forgive the toymaker who tinkered you into a doll,
who gave you a collapsible chest and a kissable mouth.
Forgive our cracked palms on your torso, our foul breath
in your lungs, forgive us as you perpetually drown,
and we can never save ourselves enough, and we have
forgotten that you always had a name.

Portrait of God as This Twelve-Year-Old Girl

God squirms against the scratch of an unnecessary bra.
God rides her bicycle to the market,
buys 50-cent chocolate bars and glass bottles of Coke.
She bleeds, and it's not the red of ladybugs.
God writes secret love letters on an old typewriter and hopes
someone and no one will read them.
God watches her grandmother die
and doubts her own existence.
God sleeps late.
God writes poems about unicorns.
God's brain is the heat and snap
of a July sparkler at dusk.
God is the night she ran away.
God reads Judy Blume and doesn't get it.
God nicks her ankle learning to shave—
her blood is the color of ladybugs and doesn't stop.
God's brain prunes synapses like sucker cane from rootstock.
When she's alone, god plays solitaire with a powdered deck,
practices walking in heels and wonders if she's beautiful.
God is beautiful.
God captures ladybugs in a jar of grass,
stabs holes in the tin lid with a kitchen knife.

Portrait of God as Ode to Panties (Remix)

Fine,
feel them. Wonder:
Would a dancin' behind
undo them? You never

see how time—
baby, girl, legs—
stays all night,
how night begs

to hold down a body:
Mine to use.
Shit. You only
want what you choose—

to do what you know
and the right to *no*.

Portrait of God as First Kiss

His name was Dustin, but she called him Dusty in her head because he was always dirty. Dusty lived in the duplex next door to the duplex where she moved with her mom and her mom's new boyfriend. Just for the summer. Sometimes she walked with Dusty to Circle K for Ice Pops, the dye staining their tongues rainbow. Dusty had a treehouse and asked if she wanted to see. She followed him up the ladder, and when he asked if he could kiss her, she said yes. She was curious. When Dusty's pale, mud-streaked face pressed against her own sunburned skin, a frog crawled down her throat and died in her belly, and after that she walked to the liquor store alone.

Portrait of God as Ruth in Boaz's Fields

For wherever you go, I will go.
        —Ruth 1:16

The sky is an ashtray of abalone shell.
Her body is the difference between *reap* and *glean*;
this is how a man paints a hungry woman.
Her arm is a pale-bellied poodle waiting for a tummy rub,
or her arm is turned needleward, awaiting nurse.
Is fear beautiful?
See also: nude model in unhearthed studio—
crocoite and zinc, root of madder, coarse linen—
her nipples dart like minnows from the net,
and the straight male artists (women are yet
still life) pretend not to want to press their mouths
like flowers against the page of her.
Maybe she'll allow that pleasure,
thinking of the soldi, her own mouth warmed
by crescentina, and thinking too of Ruth and that ridiculous
rooster tail of wheat. Ruth who marries Boaz, but what
dreams the gaze beyond the frame? Of being touched by hands
as slender as swift wings.

Portrait of God as a Woman Like That (Remix)

The night defines, friend:
Mine is a moot charade,
hard mirror. When
does the line change?

The wonder point seems
probable want—cute—
but start the long and late of me
and watch the wish cool.

Funny is a good girl;
reason, a woman's pose,
arms holding dirt,
a body the self knows.

You make of love an eye
that sees and doesn't find.

Portrait of God as Golden Shovel Ending in Poet's Own Words

after Philip Levine

Before you, Philip, I
filled my shelves with cotton candy goodbyes, was
bewitched by a confectionary heart, but at twenty-four
I wanted to have grown up with factory-gritted hands, and
kept my lines as tidy as a punch card. Had
I known you, would I have called you Philster? Mister? No
sense in peeking back at an unhappened past. No use
being afraid you'd say my poems were too fly-sweet for
anyone's good, or more like a hover outside the
empty bathroom stall: predicted disgust. God
of poetry is what I saw on that stage, and a kind of
human, also, sarcastic great uncle, small from the cheap seats. My
hands were soft and stunk of tequila—I'll be honest. Some fathers
fall through the transom and forget outside ever existed; no
doubt your sons had squabbles. No kid's ever found use
for a poet parent, or so I'm told by my own children, for
all the hours we turn to the windswept field of the page. Anything
that lets us taste our tears—with grease or honey—is spiritual,
isn't it? But here I have answered my own question.

Portrait of God as Worten's Market

Georgetown, California, population 2,500,
seems smaller with its one blink
where pickups line the center road.
We parked the Subaru and peeked
through the windows of the local bar, though
even from a distance we could see it was empty.
We wandered past the firefighters hovering
at the open mouth of the station,
found Worton's Market and inside
the scent of spiced meat and bleach, even through our masks.
No one wore a mask except my mother and me,
like the strangers we were. Everyone—
the customers talking horses, the traffic workers with buzz cuts
under hard hats waiting in the deli line—coyote eyed us.
I felt obliged to purchase gum while Mom
held her phone and showed a photo to the cashier.
She couldn't help but called out to the store,
"Anyone know this lady's sister?" and the workmen gathered
around, red-faced in their orange vests,
their unmasked breath collecting in the air, as one-by-one
they gazed at the digital image of my aunt,
asked her name, 'til one guy said, yeah,
he knew someone who knew her, sent us back to the bar,
the side door now, where we knocked, and after awhile
another man recited the number
of a woman who sometimes cleaned houses
with my aunt the next town over.
By phone, this woman took Mom's number
and said my aunt would call soon, so we waited
on a bench from where we could see the firefighters,
the traffic workers, the dimly lit bar,
and the townsfolk carrying little shopping bags

in and out of Worton's. We spoke quietly of my cousin,
the recent photos of him cycling the shoreline, his love of the sea
his baby girl, the parking garage where his body was found,
the paraphernalia, the summer my aunt carried him
low in her belly and shared my bedroom,
the years her hunger swallowed her, how it gnaws at us all,
the words heavy in my mother's mouth those few moments
before—

Portrait of God as the Artist's Regret

Nothing left of the memory but teeth,
movie grimace of mouth
white finials smeared bloody
intended to shred
sea lion or squid
and yet the fear has tree-ringed us.
Listen, I was four.
Still, I have bobbed swells
off Playa del Muertos, have lifted
my mask and gasped
in delight at the sight
of a slender sandbar swiveling its body
between my legs.
Science says great whites can be
as sweet as Mr. Rogers whose puppet voice
soothed our afternoons,
but a generation of us sat
in gash red seats
and screamed in the dark
beside people who hurt
us for real, and we could not
name the difference
as we blinked out
of the theater,
sea-legged our way back
into Datsuns and duplexes,
an empty ocean between us.

Portrait of God as Keeper of Keys

Pig Slop Girl
or
Emptier of Chamber Pots
most certainly
would have been my work.
Still, I would have liked
very much to live when
a door was unlocked
with a skeleton key—a tool
called by its metaphor. The lace
of the iron handle heavy
in my palm. The clank and scrape
of opening. The cold metal
scent of a keyhole shaped
like the black tunnel of a train
that hasn't yet arrived.
My eye pressed against its light.
I want to be the keeper of keys—
all of them clink-jangling my belt—
in a town where everyone claps
to be let in, and evening
rush hour brings a standing ovation.
I want this town to be
in heaven. What I'm saying is I want
heaven to be more than a candle
I stopped wishing on, and when you arrive—
late father, as always—
I'll sway the keys in that great
liminal space and sing
that I won't let you in,
and we'll laugh and laugh.
Neither of us will know
whether or not it's a joke.

Portrait of God as Words with Friends with Your Father's Second of Three Wives: A One Line Golden Shovel

He must have been in love with both women
at once. How could he not be?
Love strangles the hearts of even the most wise
among us, though we beg it to keep
its hands to itself. Your
father was not a wise man. His mouth
held secrets like a crooked cupboard that never quite shut—
broken hinge—which is how you know of the pregnancies. Don't
ask about the bracelet your mother found. Don't advertise
the past. Don't play *betrayal* on a triple word score. She was your
joy, and you wanted her to stay, but he wasn't that kinda man.

Portrait of God as Jolene's Response (Remix)

he calls, flaming,
voice, soft with sleep,
he talks skin and spring,
easily, easily

your pleas just there
like ivory rain
begging summer
green again

your beauty is breath, love—
beyond lock and keep—
never your cry of
compare, compete

happiness is not one whatever man
know your eyes, your only name

Portrait of God as Dysfunctional Family

There are holes in the wall the size of god's fist.
God is the wet crunch made by the cracked tab of a Budweiser
on a Saturday morning. The scent of potatoes fried in bacon fat
on Sunday mornings is god, egg whites scrambled cast iron gray.
Some days god is the vacuumed odor of the carpet
under your body where your stepbrother presses
the weight of himself.
God is a kitchen knife that misses.
God is the scatter of gravel under the tires of your mother's car.
God is a body unclutching fear.
On sick days god fills you up like quiet and grilled cheese
with onion soup.
Some evenings god tries to explain math equations.
Sometimes god is a happy drunk who plays Rolling Stones covers
into the night, and sometimes god pulls his revolver
from under his pillow.
God's intentions aren't always clear.
God doesn't care that she's a bitch.
Sometimes god is the unanswered pulse of your knuckles
against a locked door.
Sometimes god is the keyhole through which you watch
your mother smack someone who isn't you. Thank god.
God reads the dictionary like a dime store novel.
God is the ink scrawled on the letter you find torn and soggy
with coffee grounds, your name made curse.
God's voice plays through the broken radio tuned to oldies
in the hatchback your stepdad helped you buy—the god fence
he repaired after.
God belts "Love is Battlefield" in the passenger seat as you drive
out of town—last time, you swear it.
God is the *fasten your seatbelt* light on the Boeing that flies your
children home.

Portrait of God as Mother Weather

If your mother is lightning,
if the warm engine of her heart
is bittered by the chill of words on her breath,
if the cumulus tragedy of her
lashes a blaze of startle-streaked nights

be silent in the burnt canyon of your body.
Feel the universe rush its oceanself
to fill your cloven chest, wash clean
your sooted bones. Wait
for the crash of abundance.

Portrait of God as Your Mother Offering to Gift You a Gun

What if your mother named the gun Elsie?
What if firearms are the most common means
of suicide in the U.S.?
What if the gun was your grandmother's?
What if 30 years ago your mother found you in your childhood
bedroom, your mind tangled in the flowered wallpaper?
What if you have a black-and-white photo of your grandmother
standing in a field carrying Elsie, wearing mud boots, a church
dress you imagine is pink but is probably yellow.
What if you're embarrassed to say you swallowed a family-sized
bottle of Ibuprofen because it wasn't a gun?
What if your grandmother's middle name was Elsie?
What if your grandmother rarely spoke because she had
Huntington's disease, but no one knew?
What if people with Huntington's have higher suicide rates?
What if your mother found you and roused you enough to mumble
to your grandmother on the corded phone?
What if that conversation is hidden at the end of a labyrinth
you refuse to walk?
What if it's okay you didn't want to die?
What if there's no other side?
What if depression is a drunken preacher and some days still you
are filled with belief?
What if Huntington's disease is genetic, fatal and causes physical,
cognitive, and psychiatric impairment?
What if your future is a carnival coin and the silver is weighted?
What if your mind is the glint of a coin tossed and hovering?
Apex in blue sky.
What if the last words you said to your grandmother were,
I'll see you on the other side?

Portrait of God as American Assisted Living Facility

God is a dandelion woman in a cotton pink robe
who doesn't care the buttons are loose.

God is a locked door with a keypad.

An afternoon woman with smeared mascara
dances with her father;
God is the window between.

God fell down again.

The swing nurse who touches the shoulder
of the man whose mother calls him
by her husband's name—is also god.

God is an uneaten pudding cup
left behind, just in case.

The wandering, the wrestling,
the not-schizophrenic ones
swallowing Haldol to quiet the hall
are god, too.

God is a small paper cup.

God is a corner TV at top volume,
reruns of *Happy Days* in an empty room.

God is no visitors today.

She seems so familiar, thinks god,
this round-faced woman
who brings ice cream and photographs.

God is the garden wall,
espaliered apple branches.
God is climbing.

The nearest stop, less than a mile.
God is the #12 bus,
the nasal sting of exhaust.

Portrait of God as Contemplation of Suicide
While Driving Highway 80 and After Reading Pema Chödrön

Three big rigs surround us, packed tight and full with bee boxes, and through the mesh meant to protect them I watch as some bees hold to their hives, and others cling to truck metal, and many more are caught by the wind, flung against windshields where their pollen-laden bodies smack and spatter gold across the glass. My keeper husband says the pollinators tossed beyond the rushing river of vehicles will be lost without a colony to call them home, and I try, Pema, to let the sorrow blow through me, knowing even the bees that arrive at the central valley orchards will likely be contaminated and die, too, but not before dusting the blossoms that allow the tree to fruit with almond kernels and grow to fatten my favorite chocolate bars. I confess I do turn away, toward the actual river, brown and slow, the low, photogenic iron bridge in the distance, and the unhoused folks camped along the banks, and why not me, I've wondered so often, the gusts blowing hard against the hives stacked high inside my ribs, each piece of me a nameless something that cannot withstand the gales of sorrow, is dragged from the house my heart has made and wanders lost along the water's edge where there's a roofless shelter of blue sky and tarps strung from branch to bare January branch, and where someone is living a life right there on the other side.

Portrait of God as Gas Station Haiku

latch fumble, cap twist
cigarettes and chewing gum
perfume of goodbye

Portrait of God as Field Notes from a Small-Town Reporter

It's the red rectangle I notice
not the wrinkled cap,
the saltwash of his sober white face,
beard like silver ash that clings
to an untapped cigarette.
It's not until I've turned the corner
that I remember the night
this man's son drank his way to the tracks,
let the train do what a train does,
how the police ruled it suicide,
but this father, drunk on rage and whiskey,
demanded I *unwrite it*
because a family isn't a family, he said,
if a son marks his own book with death's stamp.
He was a happy boy, this father said,
and I remember the words of the conductor
through the phone line, his voice
telling what his eyes saw,
a young man who was finished with this life.
When I was young my uncle
said the railroad always gifted him
with one day off after he couldn't
stop the train in time, which was
every time, and I wondered how this conductor,
this witness, spent his one free day.
"It happened just like you wrote it," he said,
and I had to tell the father that I couldn't
unwrite the story, and I let him
scream sorrow at me, told myself to take it,
from this same man standing on the highway overpass
holding onto his MAKE AMERICA GREAT AGAIN sign
like the small boy
he once, impossibly, lifted high
while pointing to something beautiful
in a distant field.

Portrait of God as Seasons and Limits

Let's say this school is called Lakeside Meadow,
where, on the first of September,
children gather in the storynook,
sit crisscross applesauce, press
knees together and jostle
for a better view of the picture book
as the pages make their papery swishing,
hushing.

Beyond the shelter of bookshelves—
beyond the walls of this library
and wire fence lines—pastureland swoons
in each of the four directions,
grasses and live oaks, where doves migrate
and nest, feed on seeds and snails,
the doves' earth-gray feathers as soft
as the coos that greet our arrival
each day, except this one.

"It's only the doves," the principal writes
in a staff email. "It's only the opening
of hunting season."

We are not to be alarmed as the air rings
with the disconnected snap of shotgun fire
from hunters we can't see,
but who likely stalk the fields as one long, thin
snake, as they have done for generations, before
the arrival of swing sets and bright yellow circling buses.

This is a secret we cannot keep from the children.

Today in the storynook I read
a book about doves: white-winged, spotted, turtle, mourning.
The children listen, raise hands, and tell me
how to say *dove* in the languages of their homes:
paloma, ghugi, dav, gezi, golub.

The school is not called Lakeside Meadow.
I have lied to you, dear reader.
I don't need to tell you the reason.

Portrait of God as Ars Poetica with Ghosts

How many times did we discuss our pomes
while sipping coffee, corner table, nights
near windows overlooking Merritt's lights,
the winter lake itself like poetry.

Prosciutto, pasta, mascarpone, red wine,
our supper, always courses. *Bellies full
before the words,* he'd say, his apron snug
on button-down. Then, panettone, tea,

and tales of war, of Nazis. Questions held
him hostage still; the trek to Italy.
Il bel paese didn't wait, but she—
his bella signorina—later, wife—was there.

We write, and what is poetry if not
the paper boats of children, far from shore,
a little wind-torn, turning turtle—lost
among the currents, Oakland's tidal slough.

Renato's out there now, ghost gondolier
of dark—imagine—setting our boats ablaze.

III

There are a hundred ways to kneel and kiss the ground
—Rumi

Portrait of God as the Beginning

There were fifteen of us in a van
filled with desert wind.
The redhead next to me
said she had anxiety attacks
and wanted a baby.

I swore I would see Havasupai
before I settled
with yellow flowered wallpaper.

When the van stopped
and all the women squatted
behind sand hills, I couldn't pee.

We drove into the swollen night
and thought we glimpsed a baby fox
slipping across the road.
Someone sang "St. Judy's Comet"
and told stories of ants and armadillos
while I read *Animal Dreams* with a flashlight.

Finally, we slept by the canyon cliff.
Near morning I dreamed I fell
through the blood-streaked sunrise
into blue-green turtleback water.
When I opened my eyes
I knew she was with me.

Portrait of God as One Saturday in September

Our days are made of goodbyes I said
when our daughter didn't want to leave
at the end of that long summer
before she and I stuffed the Subaru
with blankets, pillows, suitcases
and pulled away slowly from the gray pines,
canals, and mandarin orchards,
drove like a freefall from the mountains
into the beach town where we found
her father waiting, where the three of us
unburdened the car of its boxes and carried
them up the stairwell to the dorm floor
where the smell of weed greeted us,
and went for lunch—the memory
of the food is gone and unimportant—
but we took photos at the cliff edge
where we could see a silver stretch of shore
and the sun following its usual path home
that told us it was time,
so we did go then, and he
drove me to the bakery
where I'd left my car,
but the bakery was closed now,
the lot lonely, and we hugged there
in the almost dark, the ocean repeating
its mantra in the background.
Good job, Mama, her father said
before we parted ways again.

Portrait of God as Daughter Cooking Ddukbokki

A long-ago lover damned our white co-workers who twisted their noses at the scent of fish sauce wafting from his lunch bowl, and I do not want to be an old racist white lady, and yet my nose doesn't care what I want because when I return home, and the house smells of anchovy and red pepper paste, my nose says *this isn't my kitchen,* and my nose is in cahoots with my mouth, I guess, because my daughter ladles the sauce she perfected with college roommates, and I taste only heat on my tongue, and now the cookware has imbibed the spice and every recipe—soups and casseroles passed down through generations—tastes unfamiliar. I keep quiet and think of Nana Ivy, my Scottish great grandmother, learning to cook the Italian stew my children cherish, and wonder whether Nana's mother turned her nose at the scent of oregano simmering on the stove, and my father's wife who taught me to make sopa Azteca with homemade tortillas. My college studio embraced chile and cilantro, the grist of future family suppers. One day perhaps my daughter will be called Nana, and her grandchildren—if crops and seas are not scoured empty—will be welcomed with fishcakes, kelp, and boiled eggs, flavors that will be the essence of home, and the children themselves may contain beautiful cacophonies of countries in their most American blood.

Portrait of God as Daughter

Back in the day
you could feel god
below your solar
plexis, a kaleidoscope
of butterflies, all shimmer
wings at flickered rest. Later,
god was drunk
on breastmilk, her droolface
swaying and pressed
against your morning
breath. God held your hand
at pedestrian crossings
and trusted your broken
sense of direction.
God bought herself a silver
Toyota. She drove it
into a blue dot
on a digital map
in your pocket. Still,
you held her close.
Now god mostly
doesn't return
your texts, except
to write, "I miss you,"
at unpredictable intervals
while you dream,
and when you wake
you're not sure
she was ever there.

Portrait of God as My Son's Epistaxis

A chickadee's egg speckled ruby.
Or, no: a bathroom sink spattered bloody.
When tweezing fine hairs, I lean close to the mirror,
Instead of my chin in the glass, a carmine smear.

The hardwood floor at dawn: chart mapping Jupiter where it goes.
A shower curtain once pastel, now watercolored brown.
The tissues trashed, a miniature murder scene in snow.
Each day my son breaks a rule to which I have been bound:

Be prepared
Be neat
Be aware
Be discreet

Cradle your blood like a secret dream, enshroud it in your hand.
Never speak, but bury it deep in the bottom of the can.

Portrait of God as the Space in My Mouth Where My Front Teeth Once Lived

The soft, succulent heart of an orange is called
the pulp, as is the tender   marsh of the tooth.
What about the pulpless? Those with an iron post,
or absence, where the heart of a tooth should be?

I grin at the mirror, the black hole in my gumline
winking back at me, and I wonder how it would be
to greet the world as many do—to take the em-dash
in my mouth to open mic night at City Hall,
uncover   my laughter.

I have learned, America, that without
these bleached white bones filling my mouth
my future is as bright as the deer carcass I pass
on the two-lane   highway I drive to work;
hourly, he is vulture-burnished.

At 13, eight was my lucky   number,
yellow striped were my roller-skates winging
neon through the basketball courts at summer dusk.
After, the asphalt. My teeth dissolving with the sunlight.

An EKG wave, squirrel gray, made cartography of my mouth.

Last night, a tooth not mine—Number 8—leapt
from my mouth again,   and I am my own fault,
the scent of shame burning like a dental drill.

My tongue in the void, I suck and fondle, kiss my hidden lip.

Look people in the eye is what I was told, but I look
people in the teeth—gapped, bashful, opalesque
and murk—to find out   what I still believe.

Portrait of God as Popcorn Kernel

Nearly broke my tooth.
It made me cry, and it made me
never want to eat again—
until there was hunger.
The tooth, a molar, was not cracked
the dentist said gleefully
and pointed at another
black and white X-ray
that never fails
to make me reflect on my mortality.
And then he poked
a very cold stick in my mouth
to make certain the nerve
still works properly.
It does, as evidenced
by my scream.
I am quite alive.
Afterward, I loudly imitated
the BWAH HA HA
I imagine echoes inside his head
as he tortures his patients.
He smiled shyly and said,
"I'm not allowed to laugh like that."

Portrait of God as Middle-Aged Woman in the Shower

For Lanci Anne Sorensen, 10/3/1971–11/7/1986

Her upper arms these days
are textured elephant ankles,
and her ass dips low
like the loose elastic band
of her favorite underwear.
The shower window—what is the purpose
of this window?—overlooks
the neighborhood,
and the neighborhood overlooks
the silhouette of god's body
as she pats down her lump-threatened
breasts and soaps the betweens.
Once, she fretted over up-the-street-boys
who circled the block
on loud, disgruntled dirt bikes
as she rinsed what
her grandmother called
her second smile, and god's heart butterflied
when solar salesmen knocked
with another unlikely pitch.
She notices now two cow spots
at the edge of her hand
where as a girl she inked eyes
to make a puppet of her side fist.
She wiggled her hand, and this friend
told jokes from a fat thumb-lip,
the same fist she wielded
in seventh-grade self-defense,
required after the body
of a missing teen was found

in nearby woods, and the officer
reminded the all-girl class
to never, ever run
from a man with a gun or leave
the door unlocked
while inside the bathroom
because no young lady is safe,
even at home.
God lifts a fresh razor
from its caddy, stretches
one fuzzy leg to the lip
of the tub, leans into the light.

Portrait of God as a Marriage Haiku

wake to Sunday storm
will our old chimney leak?
raindrops sting spring fire

Portrait of God as Damp Dish Towel

Useful and forgotten daily,
the dish towel sops milk spilled in shafts
of morning light across the kitchen table,
catches long, silver tendrils of slobber
as they dangle precariously
from the dog's hungry maw.

Not an embroidered bird-flower cloth
or even a towel handed down
from grandmothers and worn delicate,
but a plain, cotton rectangle, snipped,
maybe, from an outgrown shirt.

It hangs from the oven door or
drapes the ever-dripping faucet.
Never quite dry, yet the towel works
to unwaterlog saucepans and salad bowls
in their journey between rack and cupboard.

Once in a while you call it a rag
and remember a time when
demanding women were called rags, too,
and wonder at the origin of the epithet.

On the rag, girls used to say in school,
before those rags became small, white bullets,
and then became unnecessary—
the relief and fear over the loss
of blood, or lack of lost blood.
Menarche inversed.

You think of this
as you hold the damp dish towel
in one hand and with the other
lift a dry wineglass to your spouse
who stands before the sink, elbow-deep
in water gone cold, gone gray, soaked
in another kind of loss. *You missed a spot,*
you tell him, *right there,*
and rub your own red lipstick
from the rim.

Portrait of God as Gold Wedding Band

And it's lost in the night, and there's no moon to catch its glint, only stormclouds and wind to warn that rain is leering and you'd better get off your knees, out of this forsaken parking lot, because the streetlights are dull and flickering and that flashlight with its one wandering bulb skittering across the asphalt is no match for the starless dark and anyway you forgot your coat. All you did was that thing you do with your hands a dozen times a day, but this time something slipped—a promise—flew from your finger, the one the ancients believed led straight to the heart, but that was never true, and even if it was, what do four chambers have to do with all those vows we made? Come home.

Portrait of God as Lovemaking in the Time of Pandemic

Weeks after the fever passes, and still, I won't press
my lips to the silver stubble below your tender ear. You,
showering while I brush my teeth
before the steamed mirror,
won't swish away the flowered curtain,
or call me to the rush and wash
to cup my dry body
against the clean, warm arch of your back.
Weeks of almost kisses, near misses.
We're not greedy with our love, no more
babies to be made in this old, tired bed, sheets
frayed, soft as mouths of moths.
And then the night—your rough palm on my hipbone,
and I'm reeled from dream depths, cool and green,
like the flooded meadow where as a boy
you cast your weighted line, awake
in solitary dark mornings, bass-waiting and joyful.
We are somewhere between that deep water, ice melt
sloshing boatside, forsythia fire along the bank,
and here, this marriage, this quiet, quiet, the longing
hum, somewhere in a swirl of moonsilk, starspawn,
the stream frogs singing springtime beyond
the irises beyond the bedroom window
and we are forbidden, and we are fearful,
and we are dawn-sleeping as the sun sharpens its blade
over all of our impossible futures.

Portrait of God as My Intention to Write a Poem About the Day My Love Became a Cyborg—

Because it's so clever how each human is a steam engine, every cell a locked firebox that burns with the coal of glucose. Isn't this a terrific metaphor? The jailer pacing the raucous halls of our bodies with her jangling keys of insulin, how sometimes she unlocks every firebox at once and the pistons roar, and sometimes the skeleton keys scrape the lock but no longer fit, and what does a locomotive do when the coal car is overfull, when the coaling tower tumbles? But maybe the title of this poem should be, "The Day the Industrial Revolution Kissed the Information Age Inside My Lover's Body" because of the small needle jabbed into the soft underside of my love's furred arm and the microcomputer like a small, pale god wafer attached there. It's not more painful, he says, than a piece of giftwrap tape tugging at fine hairs. He waves the magic wand of his phone and presto: his sugar numbers appear. No more stab of fingers each morning, the odor of fresh blood mingling with the bitter scent of roasted coffee beans. *I'm in love with a cyborg,* I'd proclaim! And our body engines will barrel parallel tracks another forty years, my love guarantees, but when I ask the oracle to bless our poem—again and again— she promises only seventeen.

Portrait of God as Supermarket Haiku

beep beep beep beep beep
lost lover fondles lettuce
you found everything

Portrait of God as High-Five After Making Love

After Galway Kinnell

For he knows mornings are for me
sludge that blooms pink below the bathroom sink stopper
and prevents the tooth-pasted water from its long
meander through the house pipes.
I am the water in this metaphor.
For he is a man who wakes with joy
in his pants, presses the length of himself against
the soft flannel of my pajamas, and fervently
hopes I'll turn toward him, and we will each remove
the mouth guards that prevent stress-cracked molars in the night,
and I do, and we do, trying to be alone in the together place
while the dogs whine for kibble,
and the tabby cat has come home from its walkabout
yowling angrily to alert the neighborhood
that we have neglected his bowl. We fear
this cacophony may wake our heavy-footed teen who will stomp
to the refrigerator and moan loudly that, once again,
we are out of milk, even though he has his own
pocket change, and the market is right there.
The hot April morning blazes into our bedroom,
spotlighting our sags and wrinkles. These body husks
like spent milkweed strewn outside our window
have endured and witnessed childbirth,
stomach flu, food poisoning and injury, and yet
we suspend our disbelief a few more minutes—
or we don't and still go on—
whispering words that have not yet failed to make us
forget we are human, forget the constant tug of gravity,
the feeling that the whole world is impatient for our return,
and yet we keep it waiting.

End Notes

"Portrait of God as Ode to Panties (Remix)" : Source text: Gibbons, Billy F.; Lee Beard, Frank; Hill, Joe Michael. "She's Got Legs." *Eliminator.* Ardent Studios. 1983.

"Portrait of God as Ruth in Boaz's Fields" : Ekphrastic poem. Source: *Ruth in Boaz's Fields,* oil on canvas, Francesco Hayez, 1856.

"Portrait of God as a Woman Like That (Remix)" : Source text: Springfield, Rick. "Jessie's Girl." *Working Class Dog.* RCA, 1981.

"Portrait of God as Golden Shovel Ending in Poet's Own Words": Levine, Philip. "Words on the Wind." Edited by David Lehman and David Wagoner. *Best American Poetry*, 2009, pp. 72–72.

"Portrait of God as the Artist's Regret" : "In the years following the film's release, the number of large sharks in the waters east of North America declined by about 50 percent." – "Steven Spielberg Regrets How 'Jaws' Impacted Real-World Sharks." Jacquelyn Germain, *Smithsonian Magazine,* Dec. 20, 2022.

"Portrait of God as Words with Friends with Your Father's Second of Three Wives: A One Line Golden Shovel" : Source text: Raitt, Bonnie. "Women Be Wise." *Bonnie Raitt,* Willie Murphy, 1971.

"Portrait of God as Jolene's Response" : Source text: Parton, Dolly. "Jolene." *Jolene.* RCA, 1973.

About the Author

Patricia Caspers is the founding Editor-in-Chief of *West Trestle Review* and the author of two full-length poetry collections: *In the Belly of the Albatross* (Glass Lyre Press, 2015) and *Some Flawed Magic* (Kelsay Books, 2021). The first person in her family to attend university, she graduated from Mills College with an MFA in Creative Writing. She won the Nimrod-Hardman Pablo Neruda Prize for Poetry, was the recipient of a Hedgebrook residency, and was named the best columnist and education reporter in the state by California Newspapers Association. She is a librarian and a Unitarian Universalist.

www.ingramcontent.com/pod-product-compliance
Lightning Source LLC
Chambersburg PA
CBHW030912170426
43193CB00009BA/819